Railway Series No. 12

THE EIGHT FAMOUS ENGINES

by

THE REV. W. AWDRY

with illustrations by
JOHN T. KENNEY

KAYE & WARD LIMITED

First published by
Edmund Ward (Publishers) Ltd 1957
Ninth impression by Kaye & Ward Ltd
The Windmill Press, Kingswood, Tadworth, Surrey
1984

ISBN 0 7182 0011 X

Printed and bound in Great Britain by
William Clowes Limited, Beccles and London

DEAR FRIENDS,

The Fat Controller's engines are now quite famous. They have been on the Wireless, and had many other adventures. But he had another plan too for his engines, and this book will tell you what it was.

THE AUTHOR

Percy takes the Plunge

SOMETIMES Percy takes stone trucks to the other end of the line. There, he meets engines from the Other Railway.

One day, Henry wanted to rest in the shed; but Percy was talking to some tank-engines.

". . . It was raining hard. Water swirled under my boiler. I couldn't see where I was going; but I struggled on."

"Ooooh Percy, you *are* brave."

"Well," said Percy modestly, "it wasn't anything really. Water's nothing to an engine with determination."

"Tell us more, Percy," said the engines.

"What are you engines doing here?" hissed Henry. "This shed is for the Fat Controller's Engines. Go away.

"Silly things," Henry snorted.

"They're not silly." Percy had been enjoying himself. He was cross because Henry had sent them away.

"They are silly, and so are you. 'Water's nothing to an engine with determination.' Pah!"

"Anyway," said cheeky Percy, "I'm not afraid of water. I like it." He ran away singing,

"Once an engine attached to a train
Was afraid of a few drops of rain. . . ."

6

Percy arrived home feeling pleased with himself. "Silly old Henry," he chuckled.

Thomas was looking at a board on the Quay. It said "DANGER".

"We mustn't go past it," he said. "That's Orders."

"Why?"

" 'DANGER' means falling down something," said Thomas. "I went past 'DANGER' once, and fell down a mine."

Percy looked beyond the board. "I can't see a mine," he said.

He didn't know that the foundations of the Quay had sunk, and that the rails now sloped downward to the sea.

DANGER

"Stupid board!" said Percy. For days and days he tried to sidle past it; but his Driver stopped him every time.

"No you don't," he would say.

Then Percy made a plan.

One day at the Top station he whispered to the trucks, "Will you give me a bump when we get to the Quay?"

The trucks were surprised. They had never been asked to bump an engine before. They giggled and chattered about it the whole way down.

"Whoah Percy! Whoah!" said his Driver, and Percy checked obediently at the Distant signal.

"Driver doesn't know my plan," he chuckled.

"On! On! On!" laughed the trucks. Percy thought they were helping. "I'll pretend to stop at the station; but the trucks will push me past the board. Then I'll make them stop. I can do that whenever I like."

If Percy hadn't been so conceited, he would never have been so silly. Every wise engine knows that you cannot trust trucks.

They reached the station, and Percy's brakes groaned. That was the signal for the trucks.

"Go on! Go on!" they yelled, and surged forward together.

They gave Percy a fearful bump, and knocked his Driver and Fireman off the footplate.

"Ow!" said Percy, sliding past the board.

The day was misty. The rails were slippery. His wheels wouldn't grip.

Percy was frantic. "That's enough!" he hissed.

But it was too late. Once on the slope, he tobogganed helplessly down, crashed through the buffers, and slithered into the sea.

"You are a very disobedient engine."

Percy knew that voice. He groaned.

The Foreman borrowed a small boat and rowed the Fat Controller round.

"Please, Sir, get me out Sir, I'm truly sorry Sir."

"No, Percy, we cannot do that till high tide. I hope it will teach you to obey Orders."

"Yes, Sir," Percy shivered miserably. He was cold. Fish were playing hide and seek through his wheels. The tide rose higher and higher.

He was feeling his position more and more deeply every minute.

It was nearly dark when they brought floating cranes, cleared away the trucks, and lifted Percy out.

He was too cold and stiff to move by himself, so he was sent to the Works next day on Henry's goods train.

"Well! Well! Well!" chuckled Henry, "Did you like the water?"

"No."

"I *am* surprised. You need more determination, Percy. 'Water's nothing to an engine with determination' you know. Perhaps you will like it better next time."

But Percy is quite determined that there won't be a "next time".

Gordon goes Foreign

Lots of people travel to the big station at the end of the line. Engines from the Other Railway sometimes pull their trains. These engines stay the night and go home next day.

Gordon was talking one day to one of these.

"When I was young and green," he said, "I remember going to London. Do you know the place? The station's called King's Cross."

"King's Cross!" snorted the engine, "London's Euston. Everybody knows that."

"Rubbish!" said Duck, "London's Paddington. *I know*. I worked there."

They argued till they went to sleep. They argued when they woke up. They were still arguing when the other engine went away.

"Stupid thing," said Gordon crossly, "I've no patience."

"Stupid yourself," said Duck, "London's Paddington, PADDINGTON, do you hear?"

"Stop arguing," James broke in, "you make me tired. You're both agreed about something anyway."

"What's that?"

"London's not Euston," laughed James. "Now shut up!"

Gordon rolled away still grumbling. "I'm sure it's King's Cross. I'll go and prove it."

But that was easier said than done.

London lay beyond the Big Station at the other end of the Line. Gordon had to stop there. Another engine then took his train.

"If I didn't stop," he thought, "I could go to London."

One day he ran right through the station. Another time he tried to start before the Fireman could uncouple the coaches. He tried all sorts of tricks; but it was no good. His Driver checked him every time.

"Oh dear!" he thought sadly, "I'll never get there."

COKE

One day he pulled the Express to the station as usual. His Fireman uncoupled the coaches, and he ran on to his siding to wait till it was time to go home.

The coaches waited and waited at the platform; but their engine didn't come.

A porter ran across and spoke to Gordon's Driver. "The Inspector's on the platform. He wants to see you."

The Driver climbed down from the cab and walked over to the station. He came back in a few minutes looking excited.

"Hullo!" said the Fireman, "what's happened?"

"The engine for the express turned over when it was coming out of the Yard. Nothing else can come in or out. They want us to take the train to London. I said we would, if the Fat Controller agreed. They telephoned, and he said we could do it. How's that?"

"Fine," said the Fireman, "we'll show them what the Fat Controller's engines can do."

"Come on!" said Gordon, "let's go." He rolled quickly over the crossings and backed on to the train.

It was only a few minutes before the Guard blew his whistle; but Gordon thought it was ages!

"COME ON! COME ON!" he puffed to the coaches. "Comeoncomeoncomeon!"

"We're going to Town, we're going to Town," sang the coaches slowly at first, then faster and faster.

Gordon found that London was a long way away. "Never mind," he said, "I like a good long run to stretch my wheels."

But all the same he was glad when London came in sight.

4

The Fat Controller came into his office next morning. He looked at the letters on his desk. One had a London post-mark.

"I wonder how Gordon's getting on," he said.

The Station-Master knocked and came in. He looked excited.

"Excuse me Sir, have you seen the news?"

"Not yet.   Why?"

"Just look at this Sir."

The Fat Controller took the Newspaper. "Good gracious me!" he said, "there's Gordon. Headlines too! 'FAMOUS ENGINE AT LONDON STATION. POLICE CALLED TO CONTROL CROWDS.' "

The Fat Controller read on, absorbed.

REGIONAL MAP

Gordon returned next day. The Fat Controller spoke to his Driver and Fireman. "I see you had a good welcome in London."

"We certainly did Sir! We signed autographs till our arms ached, and Gordon had his photograph taken from so many directions at once that he didn't know which way to look!"

"Good!" smiled the Fat Controller, "I expect he enjoyed himself. Didn't you Gordon?"

"No Sir, I didn't."

"Why ever not?"

"London's all wrong," answered Gordon sadly, "they've changed it. It isn't King's Cross any more. It's St Pancras."

3

Double Header

THE Fat Controller gave Gordon a rest when he came back from London. He told James to do his work.

James got very conceited about it.

"You know, little Toby," he said one day, "I'm an Important Engine now; everybody knows it. They come in crowds to see me flash by. The heaviest train makes no difference. I'm as regular as clockwork. They all set their watches by me. Never late, always on time, that's me."

"Sez you," replied Toby cheekily.

7

Toby was out on the Main Line. The Fat Controller had sent him to the Works. His parts were worn. They clanked as he trundled along.

He was enjoying his journey. He was a little engine, and his tanks didn't hold much water, so he often had to stop for a drink. He had small wheels, too, and he couldn't go fast.

"Never mind," he thought, "the Signalmen all know me; they'll give me plenty of time."

But a new signalman had come to one of the stations.

7

Toby had wanted to take Henrietta, but the Fat Controller had said, "No! What would the passengers do without her?"

He wondered if Henrietta was lonely. Percy had promised to look after her; but Toby couldn't help worrying. "Percy doesn't understand her like I do," he said.

He felt thirsty and tired; he had come a long way.

He saw a distant signal. "Good," he thought, "now I can have a nice drink, and rest in a siding till James has gone by."

7

Toby's Driver thought so too. They stopped by the water-crane. His Fireman jumped out and put the hose in his tank.

Toby was enjoying his drink when the signalman came up. Toby had never seen him before.

"No time for that," said the signalman. "We must clear the road for the Express."

"Right," said the Driver. "We'll wait in the siding."

"No good," said the signalman, "it's full of trucks. You'll have to hurry to the next station. They've got plenty of room for you there."

7

Poor Toby clanked sadly away. "I must hurry! I must hurry!" he panted.

But hurrying used a lot of water, and his tanks were soon empty.

They damped down his fire and struggled on, but he soon ran out of steam, and stood marooned on the main line far away from the next station.

The fireman walked back. He put detonators on the line to warn James and his Driver; then he hurried along the sleepers.

"I'll tell that signalman something," he said grimly.

James was fuming when Toby's Fireman arrived and explained what had happened.

"My fault," said the signalman, "I didn't understand about Toby."

"Now James," said his Driver, "you'll have to push him."

"What, me?" snorted James. "ME, push Toby *and* pull my train?"

"Yes, you."

"Shan't."

The Driver, the Firemen, the passengers and the Guard all said he was a Bad Engine.

"All right, all right," grumbled James. He came up behind Toby and gave him a bump.

"Get on you!" he said crossly.

James' Driver made him push Toby all the way to the Works. "It serves you right for being cross," he said.

James had to work very hard, and when he reached the Works Station he felt exhausted.

Some little boys ran along the platform. "Coo!" said one, "The Express *is* late. A double header too. Do you know what I think? I think," he went on, "that James couldn't pull the train, so Toby had to help him."

"Cor!" said James and disappeared in a cloud of steam.

7

The Fat Controller's Engines

ONE evening, Thomas brought his last train to the Junction. He went for a drink.

"I'm going to the Big Station," he said to Percy and Toby.

"So are we," they answered.

"Do you know," Percy went on, "I think something's up." Toby looked at the sky, "Where?"

"Down here, silly," laughed Thomas.

"How," asked Toby reasonably, "can something be up when it's down?"

"Look!" said Thomas excitedly, "Look!"

Seven engines from the Other Railway were coming along the line.

"Hullo Jinty!" whistled Percy, "Hullo Pug!

"They're friends of mine," he explained. "I don't know the others."

Jinty and Pug whistled cheerfully as they puffed through the station.

"What *is* all this?" asked Thomas.

"The Fat Controller's got a plan," answered his Driver, "and he's going to tell it to us. Come on."

So they followed to the big station at the end of the line where all the engines had gone.

The Fat Controller was waiting for them there.

"The people of England," he said, "read about Us in the Books; but they do not think that we are real. . . ."

"Shame!" squeaked Percy. The Fat Controller glared. Percy subsided.

". . . so," he continued, "I am taking My Engines to England to show them."

"Hooray! Hooray!" the engines whistled.

The Fat Controller held his ears. "Silence!" he bellowed.

"We start the day after tomorrow at 8 a.m. Meanwhile as these engines have kindly come from the Other Railway to take your place, you will show them your work tomorrow."

7

Next day, as Annie and Clarabel were going to England too, Thomas and Jinty practised with some other coaches.

Thomas was excited. He began boasting about his race with Bertie. "I whooshed through the tunnel and stopped an inch from the buffers. Like this!"

———CRASH—The buffers broke.

No one was hurt; but Thomas' front was badly bent.

They telephoned the Fat Controller. "I'll send up some men," he said, "but if they can't mend Thomas in time, we'll go to England without him."

1

Next morning the Engines waited at the Junction. Toby and Percy were each on a truck, and Duck had pushed them into place behind Edward.

Henrietta stood on a siding. The Fat Controller had called her a "curiosity". "I wouldn't dream of leaving you behind," he said, "I'll fit you up as my private coach." She felt very grand.

Gordon, James and Henry were in front. They whistled impatiently.

The Fat Controller paced the platform. He looked at his watch. "One minute more," he said, turning to the Guard.

4

"Peep peep peeep!" whistled Thomas and panted into the Station.

Annie and Clarabel twittered anxiously. "We hope we're not late; it isn't quite Eight."

"Thomas," said the Fat Controller sternly, "I am most displeased with you. You nearly upset My Arrangements."

Thomas, abashed, arranged himself and the coaches behind Duck, without saying a word!

The Fat Controller climbed into Henrietta. The Guard blew his whistle and waved his flag.

The engines whistled, "Look out England, here we come!" and the cavalcade puffed off.

4
3

The engines stood side by side in a big airy shed. Hundreds of people came to see them, and climbed in and out of their cabs every day.

They liked it at first, but presently felt very bored, and were glad when it was time to go.

The people along their line put the flags out, and cheered them home. "We are glad to see you," they said. "Those others did their best; but they don't know our ways. Nothing anywhere can compare with our Fat Controller's Engines."

5
7
3
1
6

The Rev. W. Awdry's Railway Series

RAILWAY MAP

A new map of the Island of Sodor with a key to the places where Thomas the Tank Engine and his friends have their adventures. Designed by Clive Spong with the Rev. W. Awdry. Open size 560 × 760 mm.

THOMAS'S CHRISTMAS PARTY

Thomas, Toby and Percy plan a Christmas surprise in this new, large format picture-book for younger children. Story by the Rev. W. Awdry. Full-colour pictures by Clive Spong.

POP-UP BOOKS

Moving picture-books of eight favourite stories from the series:

Thomas the Tank Engine Goes Fishing
Bertie the Bus and Thomas the Tank Engine
Henry the Green Engine Gets Out
The Flying Kipper and Henry the Green Engine
James the Red Engine and the Troublesome Trucks
Thomas the Tank Engine and the Tractor
Percy the Small Engine takes the Plunge
Henry the Green Engine and the Elephant